T. *is a Gift*

from

_____

to

_____

on the occassion of

_____

date

_____

A WOMAN TO REMEMBER

V 1.2

GRACE EPAMBA

A Woman to Remember V 1.2
© 2016, Grace Epamba

ISBN 978-1-945055-22-5

 PIRACY IS THEFT

Published by

KING'S WORD PUBLISHING

For your questions and publishing needs, write to:

E.C. Nakeli
40 S Church st
Westminster, MD 21157
E-mail: ecnakeli@yahoo.com

Printed in the United States of America

Contents

DEDICATION

*This book is dedicated to the
Champion of the Church
– The Lord Jesus Christ.*

He is the ideal MAN for all women.

Acknowledgements

My sincere gratitude for the production of this book goes to the following: - My son, Fred Misodi who committedly worked late nights to type and retype the manuscript to prepare it for publication.

My daughter and friend, Gwen who has stood with and by me at all times, encouraging me behind the scenes to fulfill my destiny. My niece Linda Motuba, a quiet but faithful prayer partner when things were challenging.

My daughter Mercy Manga and her husband Ebot who relentlessly inspired me to believe in God and His promises through their medical attention and other needs.

My daughter Loveline who also provided me with a quiet environment and medical supervision in times of health crisis. Pastor Kayode Tadese of Abundant Life Church in Cleveland, Ohio, whose book "You Will Not Go Back Empty" was an inspiration of hope. Sister Yetty Adepegba of Inspiration House RCCG London whose worship music lifted my spirit into worship as I wrote.

To you Sister Prisca Fomum, Ida Gwan and Mama Monica Atogho, I thank you for prophetically praying for me before and during the writing of this book. Pastor and Mrs Ayong for ceaseless prayer and communication, during my stay in the US where I wrote this book. Thank you all for being involved.
And to you my beloved Barbara Ma, the Lord bless you for your offer to proof read the manuscript.

Preface

The Bible is filled with the names of prominent women who lived in an era or generation different from today. In spite of the difference in their culture and background, there are valuable lessons to be learnt that can shape today's women. The women were not all great, neither were they perfect but they fulfilled God's plan for their lives in different ways as God purposed for them. Let us look at it in this way.

The Lord God chose five women of seemingly poor reputations to be part of the lineage of His Son, Jesus Christ. In Matthew 1:3-7 and verse 16, there is a record of the genealogy of the Lord Jesus Christ from Abraham to King David to which Joseph, Mary's husband belonged. To the Jews, Joseph was supposedly Jesus' real father. That is why Joseph's background was exposed to show who Jesus' ancestors and great-great grandparents were.

In this passage, Tamar's name appears. She pretended to be a harlot and enticed her father-in-law to have sex with her and even conceived. Rahab was a professional prostitute, a Gentile and non-Jew from Jericho. Bathsheba, David's wife was an adulteress who got married to her husband's murderer (David killed Uriah). Ruth was a foreigner and a descendant from Moab, a city founded on incest where two daughters had children with their father (Lot and his daughters). Mary was a young girl who got pregnant before marriage and not by her fiancée.

It is exciting and encouraging to know that God does not look at who we are, what we were in the past, where we come from, what our profession is or was, not even our reputation, whether good or bad, before He saves us. The choice is His and not man's choice. His love, compassion and mercy reach out to everyone regardless of colour, race or tribe.

Whenever I think of these women as descendants and associations of the Lord Jesus Christ, I am humbled at God's sovereignty and divine love. There is really no one that is exempted from His love, mercy, forgiveness and salvation. No one is so sinful or so bad that God cannot accept, change or use for His glory. Many of us like to be associated with or related to people of renown, those who are influential in society, those with good reputations and approved by the world's standards. We want to relate with those who can channel our interests and speak on our behalf. But the Lord of Glory came for all mankind whether good or bad in the eyes of man.

He has not changed. He wants to identify Himself with us in our plight, our circumstances, our reputation, our disappointments, misery, rejection and our disgrace. He is Love, unconditional love; not because of what we have done or not done but inspite of what we have or have not done. He wants to give meaning to our lives and change us into worthy and respectable women in society, women who can be remembered not because of their beauty, wealth or social standing but because of their godly lives and service to the Him.

Such are women of influence who transformed by the power of God, maintained a continuous and growing intimate relationship with the Lord Jesus Christ. They may not be known by the world but are known by God.

They walk with God and make themselves available to be used in order to accomplish His purposes on Planet Earth. These women have had crisis and challenges in life but they will not allow such to make them waver or give up their commitment to obey God. Always, they have had to make two choices as they faced these challenges – either to turn their backs to God and handle their lives in their own way or focus on God and turn to Him for solutions and direction. They learn, submit to God's dealings, share their experiences and impart the wisdom they have received from their training in His school of discipline to influence their generation. They make mistakes but use them to get closer to God for correction and guidance. They stand the test of the storms of life.

Any woman can be remembered by the choices she makes in life. First and foremost, to accept the one way provided by God to be reconciled to Him through His only begotten Son, Jesus Christ and become His child (John 1:12-13) or struggle to change herself by following a set of religious rules in order to please God. His way is simple. The choice is yours!

The five women mentioned in this book faced different circumstances but had one thing in common. They chose to submit to God and His ways. They all loved the Lord and overcame every mountain or hindrance that would have blocked them from going on with Him. By their choices, they each fulfilled God's purpose for their lives and have influenced many lives. Their names are remembered among other women with goals accomplished in spite of their handicaps.

What did these women have in common? Nothing but God! The Lord God transformed their circumstances into triumph.
The end result was victory, peace, joy, contentment, fulfillment and rest. This is what the Lord Jesus is in the business of doing today for women who are facing the challenges of life.

He is indeed **THE IDEAL MAN FOR ALL WOMEN.**
Follow me as we look at how it all happened!!

CHAPTER
ONE

MARY

CHAPTER ONE MARY

Many of us know Mary only as the mother of our Lord. The questions we should ask are "Why was she the one chosen? What did she do to deserve such a lofty position? What can we learn from her that can positively affect our lives? She was not the only Jewish girl in the small town of Nazareth. She was certainly not the only virgin. Also, bringing a child into the world or rather giving birth is the normal thing for women. True, hers was no ordinary child but she was a normal girl like others. The only woman who came into the world without sin was Eve, because she was created by God Himself. Unfortunately, she was the one who introduced sin into the world and lured her husband, Adam to disobey God. Sin generated into all of their offspring and Mary was no exception. So it was not because she was perfect or sinless; she was simply God's choice. God chose her for a special mission on earth, a special assignment that was uniquely hers.

The Bible does not tell us that Mary did anything to make God choose her for the business of carrying His Son. She did not know that such a thing existed in God's mind. All we know about her is that she was engaged to be married to Joseph. From what we can detect, she was still living with her parents in their home waiting for the day of her wedding. Then came the encounter with the angel carrying the message from God:
"Hail, thou art highly favoured; the Lord is with thee. Blessed art thou among women". (Luke 1:28)

Of course she was both frightened and embarrassed. She had never in her life seen an angel. She had neither heard nor received a direct message from God. What did He see in this young girl to specifically want her to encounter His presence? God looks and sees our hearts, our attitudes towards Him and His Word, which is always instructive. God can talk to us through any means He desires. It can be through an angel, a book, the Bible, through His servants, a dream or any other way He knows will touch our hearts. What is important is whether we are willing to listen.

Mary was troubled, in confusion, fearful of what to do, but ready to understand. The angel saw her frightened face and eased her fear with the encouraging words, *"Fear not."* When God's word comes to us, it is not to condemn, threaten or frighten us. He comes to speak to us with love, encouragement or peace. He also instructs us on what to do and how to do what He has instructed. He does not keep us in the dark or in ignorance of what He wants us to do. His word convicts us and does not condemn us.
And so the message continued when Mary was calm;

"Behold thou shalt conceive in thy womb and bring forth a son and thou shalt call his name Jesus. He shall be great and shall be called the Son of the Highest; and the Lord God shall give unto Him the throne of His father David. And He shall reign over the house of Jacob forever; and of His Kingdom there shall be no end."Luke 1:31-32

This was Mary's assignment; Be pregnant, deliver a child, name the child herself, and then God would take care of the rest as far as who or what the child would be. This was a strange assignment and once more she was confused and so asked the angel,
"How shall this be seeing that I know not a man?"Luke 1:34

I have asked myself why she did not think or assume that this conception could happen when she would be formally wedded to Joseph her fiancé. But in the Jewish tradition of those days, marriages were arranged by parents. The bride-to-be was kept in her parents' home until she was ready for her husband to come and take her away. As she heard the urgency in the tone of the angel, she wondered how this could happen. To her it was good news but very premature.

Our God is not the Author of confusion. He had it all figured out. The birth of His Son would have nothing of human glory. It was a matter between God and Mary. Man would have no part in it. The power of conception was from above not from a man.

Mary believed that the message was from God because it was given to her by an angel from God. She listened carefully and wanted to know more, which explains why she asked questions. From her tone, it was not because she was arguing but she was seeing things with the natural eye – the impossibility of conceiving and bearing a child without any sexual relationship with a man.

When you receive an assignment from God, you do not just hurriedly go and start doing it. It is very necessary to find out the details – when, how, what am I to do? There is always an inner conviction or compulsion that tells you, this is from the Lord. He can use dreams, His Word, one of His servants or the Ministry of the Holy Spirit into your spirit to show you how He wants you to serve Him. Sometimes He can tell you to be part of someone's ministry and to work in partnership with Him. Sometimes, it can be a distinct call. Our attitude towards the Word of God matters. If we are not committed to obeying His Word in small and big matters, and are prone to despising the teachings from the Word, it will not be possible to receive an assignment. Even though you are one of the favoured people by right of salvation, God will hardly entrust you with a specific assignment. This is part of the reason why God chose Mary.

Her humility to listen attentively, her desire to know and be taught, among many other qualities that will be exposed about her character in subsequent encounters attracted God's eye. Finally, the angel explained everything to her,

"The Holy Ghost shall come upon thee, and the power of the Highest shall overshadow thee; therefore also that Holy thing which shall be born of thee shall be called the Son of God. For with God nothing shall be impossible". Luke 1:35

Everything was clear. She got the complete message; no more questions. Mary now understood. God had spoken. She never gave it a second thought because the matter was settled. She was oblivious of the risks involved. For example, what would people, most of all her parents, say? She would be a disgrace to the family. Secondly what would happen to her engagement to Joseph? He would never get married to her because he would conclude that she had a secret lover besides him; a lover who had made her pregnant. Thirdly, according to the Jewish law, she had to be stoned to death for destroying her virginity before marriage. Yes, Mary did not consider all these consequences. To her, God's word, His command and commission was final. He must be obeyed. All fear was gone and fright gave way to yielding. She was peaceful and at rest. The humble response came out of this obedient and submissive girl:

"Behold the handmaid of the Lord; be it unto me according to thy Word." Luke 1:38

With this confirmation, the angel of the Lord departed from her. His message was received and accepted. God's Word had gone forth and was believed by the one He had chosen. There was joy in heaven.

Let me ask you some questions:
a. When did God last speak to you?

b. When did you surrender your rights to Him?

c. When did you yield to very difficult demands from the Word of God?

d. When did you take the risk to obey the Lord in spite of the consequences and public opinion?

e. When did you forget yourself and your society in order to obey God?

f. When God comes looking for a woman who will obey Him in all things in spite of what people say or what she might lose, will He find you?

These are all questions each one of us has to confront if we want to become God's handmaidens. Most times, we enjoy doing the most comfortable and convenient things when serving the Lord. We choose the things that make no demands on our personal time, our own programs, our families, our money, our life-styles, etc. Usually, anything that tampers with our projects, even if it is for the sake of the Kingdom of God, is not welcome. God who looks at our hearts and attitudes towards His work will quietly leave us alone and look for someone else who is willing and available.

Mary fulfilled the angel's, *"Blessed art thou among women".(Luke 1:28)*. There is blessedness in obedience. When God is with you, you are blessed. You enjoy His protection, provisions, promotions (not worldly promotions only), favour and many other spiritual riches.

As the angel said, *"With God, nothing shall be impossible". (Luke 1:37)*. Because of God's blessings and favour, the impossible situation of the consequences of her decision was evident. God arrested Joseph in his decision to abandon her. The angel of the Lord appeared to him in a dream and instructed him not to disown her and gave him almost the same message about the birth of the Lord Jesus. There was neither room for the Jews to stone her nor for her parents to be ashamed of her.

When we obey God and His Word or instructions He protects us. He makes us find favour before those whom we have to deal with. He stands by us and protects us against our enemies. He ensures that the purpose for which we are called is accomplished. He Himself removes the barriers and obstacles, and brings people along our way that will help us. In the pathway of obedience, God never leaves us alone.

Mary as a Disciple

Mary's humility was exposed in the way she handled her encounter with God. This thing was too big for her to carry alone. The revelations, the experiences and the message were all too much for her to handle alone. The girls around her were as inexperienced in the things of God as she was. Normally, living with her biological Jewish mother, Mary had noticed that she was not mature in the ways of God so she could not get help from her either. The Bible tells us that,

"Mary arose in those days and went into the hill country with haste into a city of Judea and entered into the house of Zacharias and saluted Elizabeth".(Luke 1:39)

What wisdom! Those who want God and want to make spiritual progress always know those who can help them. God does not want us to travel the journey of salvation alone. He wants us to be related to Him and to others who are ahead of us. Not everyone can lead us God-ward. When He sees that our hearts are hungry for Him and we are humble enough to learn from others and to submit to them, He directs us to the right person who can build us up to become mature in the ways of God. Some people call them mentors, others, disciple-makers. Whatever name you choose, they serve the same purpose. No woman can make it all by herself. The deception that you have only Jesus, your Pastor or your Church is the devil's lie. We all need personal spiritual guidance.

Without doubt, Mary had observed Elizabeth's godly pursuits and devotion from her young age. Even though they did not live in the same city, she must have established a relationship with this godly, old woman. She had seen and heard of her life with a priestly husband, her love for God and her services to Jehovah. This is where God led her to go. Notice, she did not go to Zacharias the spiritual leader but to his wife. The safest disciple-maker or mentor for any woman is another woman except in rare cases. The reasons are obvious. It also has nothing to do with age, beauty or wealth. The questions should be, *"What spiritual impartation can I get from her? Do I love or admire her way of life? Can she inspire me to follow the Lord?"* As proof that she had gone to the right person, Elizabeth prophetically confirmed the angel's message, even though she did not know that Mary was coming to visit her. Her mentor was really in touch with God.

Mary was the first woman to be filled with the Holy Spirit because the child she was carrying was the Son of God. Elizabeth's prophetic word brought light into her ignorance and she knew who she was. Overwhelmed by the lofty position to which God had promoted her, Mary joyfully expressed her feelings in worship: *"My soul doth magnify the Lord and my spirit hath rejoiced in God my Saviour."– Luke 1: 46-47*

Mary was amazed at the ways of God, to choose her from among so many other girls with wealthy backgrounds and popular families. What had she done to deserve such honour from God to be the carrier of His Son? Nothing! God merely looked down on earth and singled her out. Her gratitude could only be expressed in worship.

Have you ever sat down and contemplated on what God has done for and in you? To be chosen as a carrier of His Holy Son, to become His child by virtue of whom you are carrying? We did nothing, you merited nothing, you were not the best girl or woman, and you were not without sin. Each one of us had a past sinful life. But God looked down on earth and released His Holy Spirit to locate you and convict you unto repentance, and gave you salvation. My sister, if you find it difficult to thank God for anything, thank Him for your salvation. It is more than anything the world can offer you. To become a child of God is the highest position. You are favoured!

Once more, the humility of this young girl is seen in her behavior. She did not run back immediately to testify to the whole community or her parents about what had happened to her; after all, everything was confirmed. Her heart was after God, not after favours or blessings.

She stayed with Elizabeth for about three months. Mary wanted to be around Elizabeth to learn more and see how the practical issues and daily routines of life were handled; remember that Elizabeth too was pregnant. If God could make an old woman pregnant, then she could also learn from her how to handle the new experience of pregnancy and childbirth. Mary was not in a rush to go away because of her promotion.

Many of us have the tendency of becoming independent when God gives us a ministry or an assignment. We think we can now handle things only with God and forget those who nurtured us into maturity. We have those who look up to us but we have no-one to look upto in the human perspective. It is true that our final Authority is the Lord Jesus Christ by the help of the Holy Spirit. Nevertheless, the Lord expects us to be related to some of His servants who are ahead of us so that we do not become puffed up with pride. Mary passed that test and it had a lot of influence on her life after that.

Mary is transformed by Her Son

Finally Mary became Joseph's wife although she never had any sexual relationship with him until after the Lord Jesus was born. God later on did not speak to her concerning the Child; He only spoke to Joseph. She became his protégée and he took all the decisions for the protection of the Child. Joseph taught the Child business skills and trained Him in the profession of a carpenter, and together they thus served the community. The Jews thought that Jesus was simply the son of a carpenter. However, throughout the Bible, even though it was Joseph who was directed by God on how to protect Him from Herod's anger, it is written, *"The young child and His mother"*, *(Matt 2:13,14,20,21)* not Joseph's son. The Lord Jesus had no biological father but He was raised in a home and a family, with Mary's other four boys, (Simon, James, Judas and Joses) and several sisters. While at home for 30 years, His mother observed Him and knew that this was no ordinary child. She learnt to respect Him with awe and reverence. All she did was ponder and meditate about His behavior and *"kept these things in her heart."* Luke 2:9

As true handmaidens of the Lord, we are called to meditate, reflect and ponder over the things we hear and read in God's Word. Mary's attitude towards Jesus was transformed because of what she saw in Him at home, the words that she heard Him speak and how He related to His brothers and sisters. No wonder she hardly took offence at Him. For example, when she asked Him to solve the problem of the finished wine at the wedding in Canaan, He called her *"Woman"* instead of *"Mother"*. When she and her other sons came to look for Him when He was ministering, He openly denounced her saying, *"Who is my mother and brother?"* Can you put yourself in her place and guess how you would have reacted? She did not answer back or take offence. She had learnt to submit to Him. She had seen His wisdom, His devotion to God even at the age of twelve years, His godly nature and the miracles He had performed. That is why she approached Him for a solution at the wedding in Canaan with confidence.

Mary the Intercessor (John 2:1-11)

There was a problem at the wedding in Canaan. The wine got finished before the party ended. What an embarrassment to the host. The master of ceremony was confused and probably there was no money to buy more drinks. The guests were becoming restless, disgruntled and thinking of leaving. Mary had accompanied Jesus with His disciples to the wedding. In her quiet but observant personality, she noticed the confusion and knew that something was wrong. She decided to save the situation by going to the One who had the solution.

As we know, she knew who Jesus was. She had seen His supernatural acts at home, His strange but excellent character, His powerful declarations, prophetic utterances and wisdom which always brought solutions to family problems. She knew Him intimately, having lived with Him for about 30 years. She knew the power He possessed. She knew that He could unravel the embarrassing situation. Because of this intimate relationship she had with Him, she had the liberty to make her request, fully convinced that He would do something.

In spite of the spiteful and disrespectful answer she received from her son, "Woman, what do I have to do with you?"John 2:4. She took no offence, neither was she discouraged. Let me ask you these questions before we continue: Are you intimate enough with Jesus to believe that He will answer your request? Do you get easily irritated or stop asking when your prayer is not answered immediately and so give up? Only you can answer the questions for yourself. Mary's attitude in this particular incident can help us start again. There is hope!

Mary told the servants, *"Whatever He tells you to do, do"*. John 2:5. That's the secret – Obedience. Obey Him regardless of your feelings or misgivings. The ways of the Lord are often strange. As an intercessor (for this is what she was doing) we must be open and allow the Lord to work or answer the way He decides. Mary was not requesting anything for herself. She was a selfless woman who was not concerned only for things in her interest. She interceded for a miracle to happen, for the benefit of the bride and bridegroom. Many people did not know what had transpired behind the scenes except the servants who filled the water pots with water. Water became wine. The disciples were oblivious of what was going on. The ceremony continued and everybody in attendance - the guests, the couple, and the master of ceremony – enjoyed the best wine, as could be heard from the comments.

Someone had stood in the gap. Someone had interceded and moved the Lord to act. A woman who was burdened enough to persist for the welfare and joy of others had interceded. Yes, it was not known in public, but her work in the background brought gladness to the community. That was the fruit of her travail. She was not a public figure but her ministry of intercession was publicly rewarded.

Do you specialize in always praying for yourself, your family, children or things that will benefit you alone? Do you always make known how you prayed and God answered? Yes; you can say it is a testimony, which is good; but also pray for miracles for which only God will receive the glory. Dare to be intimate with Jesus and you will see Him do miraculous things in answer to your prayers. Be an intercessor. Ask the Lord to give you a burden for others. You will be happy when you see them rejoice because God has answered your prayers on their behalf.

Wounds of the Soul

"Yea, a sword shall pierce through thy own soul also, that the thoughts of many hearts may be revealed."– Luke 2:35

This prophecy to Mary concerning her Son was fulfilled at the death of the Lord on the cross. She had the agony of seeing her first-born Son tormented, beaten, stripped naked, spat upon, crucified with nails on His hands and feet, and publicly displayed on the cross as if He was a criminal. No mother has ever borne such pain in her heart. Nothing is mentioned about the whereabouts of Joseph – Probably he had died because he would surely have stood by his wife as he stood from the beginning of Jesus' conception and birth. She was all alone, no husband and no first Son. The Lord Jesus had to assign His beloved disciple John to take care of His mother.

Mary was hurt, broken-hearted and her soul pierced. She faced the temptation of hating those who killed her Son. She could have cursed them and borne bitterness in her heart against these people for treating her Son so wickedly and ungratefully despite all the good He had done for them. Yet in all this, there is no mention of a word of retaliation, threat, curse or complaint. She bore the agony, watching with pain and anguish of heart the scene of crucifixion, unable to do anything. What a woman!

Our souls consist of our feelings and emotions. When we are hurt, treated badly, rejected or abused in one way or the other, our attitude determines whether the soul is wounded or whether it is strong enough to make us withstand the hurt and remain calm. This happens when we also have a strong spirit energized by the Holy Spirit because of our Christ-like nature. When Christ fills our lives and we begin to resemble Him in character, our attitude towards those who hurt us is Christ-like. We forgive, we continue loving, and we don't murmur or complain. We are at peace with God. We accept everything as from a loving Father as was said of Jesus on His cross experience: *"Yet it pleased the Lord to bruise Him"*. But when our souls are wounded, the attitude is different. We are bitter against those who hurt us. We harbour unforgiving thoughts, hatred, grumbling and want to avenge the hurt. Not so with Mary; she passed the test and Satan could not cause her spirit to be defiled or attack her body.

Let me put it this way; when our soul is wounded because of our attitude towards those who have hurt us, the feelings and emotions that come out are anger, bitterness, hatred, unforgiving thoughts, and most often, self-pity. The devil now has authority and access to afflict our bodies. You see, the spirit influences our soul and the soul influences the body. When the Holy Spirit fills our lives, He makes our souls strong and our bodies are protected. When our soul is wounded, the devil has access to inflict our bodies with diseases because he sees his character in us. In effect, we become one with him in attitude and character. Most of the diseases common to women are as a result of the wounds – arthritis, fibrosis, stress, etc. The common attitudes of jealousy, envy, gossip, slander and strife weaken our spiritual maturity because of demonic defilement. When a person's soul is wounded, his mind is confused; he takes wrong decisions, mingles with wrong company and loses focus.

The way out is to repent, ask the Lord to forgive you and take time to forgive everyone who has hurt you – both believers and non-believers. Forgive yourself and plead the Blood of Jesus over your emotions, mind and thoughts, and ask the Lord to heal your soul. Many of us have sick and wounded souls and the Lord is willing to give us wholesome healing of our spirit, soul and body. If you are healed physically but your soul is still wounded, you are still in bondage. Take stock of your attitude towards people and get your deliverance today. Receive the resurrection power from above and overcome all the power of the Enemy over your soul. Do not remain in darkness or under the bondage of Satan's deception that all is well when you are carrying wounds all over your soul. When your soul gets healed, your mind gets clearer and you have a better understanding of God's Word. You will enjoy reading it and you will easily forgive and love people. Try it; it works.

Back to our sister Mary; she was victorious over the agony that she went through. She stood with her Son throughout the trials and pain while He was on the cross. She was there until He died. She was spiritually strong and stable. She believed that Jesus' declaration that He will rise again would come to pass. She identified herself with His disciples and was there at Pentecost when the Holy Spirit fell upon them and they spoke in tongues.

Nowhere was she found boasting about her Son or exalting herself above other women because of her God-given position. Her life of humility and Christ-likeness was a true reflection of God's work in a life yielded and devoted to Him. Amen!

CHAPTER
TWO

ELIZABETH

CHAPTER TWO ELIZABETH

Her story is told in Luke 1: 5-63. She was from a priestly background and the first impression we have of her is that she was barren and past the age of bearing children. Later on, she became the mother of John the Baptist, the last of the Old Testament prophets. She was one of the most faithful and devoted women of the Word. Her life has influenced many women because of her steadfast and unshakeable faith in Jehovah. She pursued God whole-heartedly in spite of her unfavourable circumstances in life. Come along with me as we explore how this great woman impacted her generation so much that her name appears in the Bible as a woman to be remembered.

Her name, Elizabeth actually means 'WORSHIPPER' or 'God is my oath'. She lived with her husband, Zachariah and both of them served the Lord. The Bible says *"They were both righteous before God walking in the all the commandments and ordinances of the Lord, blameless."Luke 1:6* What a compliment! It means they were living a life that pleased God by obeying all revealed truths and were submissive to the will of God in all things. Without any doubt therefore, Elizabeth, like her husband was a spiritual leader. She had spiritual influence in the congregation which her husband was leading and also had authority with God as an individual. In my own understanding, spiritual leadership is a result of obedience to the Word of God and obeying those whom God has put over us. It could be your husband, your local church leader, your boss in the office or anyone over you in the spiritual, professional or political set-up. A person can be appointed to a post and have responsibilities but if such an appointee lives in continuous disobedience to the Word of God or to God-given instructions from those in authority (unless they contradict God's Word), he will be demoted before God. It will not take long for God to strip such a person of all spiritual influence.

When we talk of disobedience to God's Word, we mean deliberate disobedience to what you know you should do. This is called iniquity – doing something you know is wrong and continuing in it. It grieves the Holy Spirit and blocks our spiritual receptability and intimacy with God. Obedience is a personal decision which God honours and for which He gives grace to continue in.

Her Obedience

Being the wife of a spiritual leader is not an easy task. If she had shown any insubordination she would not have been called 'blameless'. As a priest, Zachariah had the responsibility of spiritual preparation before going into the Holy of holies on behalf of the people. If he went in sin, he would not come out alive. At such times, he was expected to be alone, as all leaders of God spend time to prepare for ministry. At such times, Elizabeth must have also supported him in the background with prayers, while attending to her domestic chores and home management. She made sure she was also spiritually connected to God so that she would be in spiritual harmony with her husband. This explains why there was no conflict when it came to the God-revealed name of their son, John. They both knew he was no ordinary child so they liberated him to dwell in the wilderness as was ordained by God. When her neighbours wanted to argue with her concerning the name and thought that her dumb husband would oppose, he confirmed it – *"His name is John." Luke 1:63*

This aspect of a leader's wife is very important. No woman should hide behind her husband's spiritual position without knowing God herself. Every woman must find time to spend alone with God. Some complain of no time because of children and housework. God did not give us children as a burden or obstacle to becoming intimate with Him. We always find time for everything that is important to us. It is a matter of desire and choice. No person's relationship with God is inherited or transferred to someone else. Each person must work out his own salvation to establish his position with God. Of course, this goes for every woman who is a believer and wants to be used by God. God has no favourites. When we seek Him, we will find Him.

The second thing that comes forth is that Elizabeth was a woman with a Christ-like spirit. The grace of God was upon her. Grace is the divine ability to be and do what is naturally impossible. One would have thought that a woman who had served God so faithfully and remained in leadership for so long would have been blessed with the gift of a child. The normal attitude would have been to take offence at God, to murmur or complain to God for forgetting her. But nowhere are we told that she murmured or withdrew from serving God. Nowhere did she grow cold or discouraged.

Surely she must have been ridiculed about her faith by unbelievers. Her neighbours must have mocked her; and maybe even some believers had gossiped about her spirituality that she did not bear physical benefits. By the grace of God, she chose not to defile her spirit and lose fellowship with Him by getting angry or wallowing in self-pity. She was mature enough to demonstrate a Christ-like attitude. Her trust and confidence in God did not depend on gifts or blessings; her knowledge of Him was more important to her than His blessings. That is why she was at rest even without a child, calm and satisfied with God. She found her fulfillment in ministering to Him in quietness. Unlike Hannah who wept in much anxiety (which is normal for every woman), or Sarah who became impatient with God and took matters in her hands by giving her husband another wife, Elizabeth remained calm until God's visitation. It is not that she and her husband did not pray, because the angel of the Lord said to Zacharias, *"Thy prayer is heard"*, but there was no fretting and no restlessness. God had heard their prayers and they let go of their burden.

The point I want to bring out is that we must understand that God has His time and season to answer prayers that are in His will. We cannot bribe Him with tears or quotations from the Bible. We cannot manipulate Him to suit our own time-table. When He wants to do something of lasting impact, He creates an atmosphere where only faith wins the day.

The answer comes when no one can receive the glory, when everything looks dismal and seemingly impossible. God is very jealous of His glory and so sometimes He has to wait for His own time. What I have learnt is that prayer is not necessarily to receive, good as that is, but that it is beneficial for fellowship with God, to know His will about the request at hand and then ask with confidence because one is in harmony with Him. Sometimes, He delays to help us get rid of a particular attitude like pride or bitterness, and then after repentance, He can answer us. So there is hope for you, my sister. God has not forgotten. Keep serving; He has a surprise for you.

Elizabeth may have even given up the idea of conception because she was already too old, but God's time does not get old, neither is He ever late. He had determined from the foundation of the world to take away her reproach and reward her faithfulness on this side of Planet Earth. Let us see how she handled His miracle.

The Final Explosion

"And after those days his wife Elizabeth conceived and hid herself five months saying: 'Thus hath the Lord dealt with me in the days wherein He looked on me to take away my reproach among men."– Luke 1: 24-25

Finally God showed up in answer to the long awaited prayer. The Lord did a great thing for Elizabeth and she was going to have a baby in her old age. The normal thing most of us would have done would have been to testify in church and everywhere (which is good). Not so for Elizabeth. Her reaction and response were proof that her pursuit and service to God were not for blessings. He was her Father and she admired Him. He meant all to her. Her love for Him made her always be in His presence for growing intimacy. The pregnancy gave her an opportunity to get even closer. She immediately decided to resort to privacy and spent more time alone with Him instead of with people who would suddenly have begun visiting her, praising her and making her feel as if she were a wonder.

That is the problem with miracles. They are good for us as blessings from God but the way we handle them is important. We can end up loving and running after miracles more than the Giver of miracles. As a child of God, do not be satisfied just with the miracles from God. Do everything to know His Word, shutting out every noise and activity so that He can speak to you.

When He does, He will show you what to get rid of in your life that hinders your maturity. He will reveal truths that need to be applied to your own personal life. He may teach you how to relate to people and how to handle your home, children or your occupation, i.e., a job or some business. I see many women attracted to places of miracles but not interested in the ministry of the Word. If you practice spending even ten to fifteen minutes faithfully everyday alone with God, your love for His presence will increase and the times of meeting will also increase. He is the God who says, *"Seek me and you will find me if you seek me with all your heart." Jeremiah 29:13.* May the Lord help us to change our hearts' desire from looking for miracles to first looking for God. In this way when miracles or blessings come, the response will not end with emotional excitement but with deep sense of gratitude and awe and reverence for God that will send us withdrawing into His presence to worship and to give Him thanks as a personal Father.

Fears Released

One may ask what Elizabeth was doing in seclusion for up to five months when God blessed her. This was certainly not the first time she was spending time alone with God. She obviously had practiced being in the presence of God all her life and could never get bored even if she was without human company. She had experienced the joy of His companionship and strength. The word of God says "In returning and rest shall ye be saved; in quietness and in confidence shall be your strength". Isaiah 30:15. That word was alive in her. She had learnt how to bring her concerns first to God before making them known to man. Without pretence, she probably had fears on how to deliver a child at such an age when her youthful strength had abated. Only God could give her the strength and feminine skill. She also needed to find out how to nurse a child when maybe her breasts had already shrunk. Having been told that she was going to give birth to a boy, she must have wondered where she would have the energy to run after a young boy with youthful excesses, her husband also being an old man. She was faced with the practical preparations and domestic adjustments. She was accustomed to a home of two; but now there was going to be a new and permanent arrival whose presence would demand commitment to other pursuits. She did not take the matter lightly being carried away by seeking advice from left and right. Her priority was to seek advice from God. She needed to pray.

Of course, there were also spiritual implications to handle. Elizabeth knew that this was a child with a mission from God as announced by the angel and with strange instructions as specified in Luke 1:14-17. This was God's own boy who was coming in the spirit and power of Elijah, the Old Testament prophet. These things were too complicated for her to handle alone. Unlike the young girl Mary who did not know God and needed someone who could help her know Him, Elizabeth had learnt to hear His voice and be influenced by His presence. And so the five months were not boring. Many things had to be sorted out with God alone first before she met people. She was so soaked in His presence that when Mary who was carrying the Baptizer into the Holy Spirit approached, Elizabeth was immediately filled and the spiritual environment affected the child in her womb, who was also baptized before he was even born. After this encounter with the Lord Jesus whom Mary was carrying, all fear left her; she rejoiced and prophesied. Her confidence in God was restored. Her spirit was lifted. She was now ready to face all that God had assigned for her. Hallelujah! She had peace.

Try it, my sister! Carry out constant visits alone with Him. Tell Him your fears, ask Him for help and guidance, go there and express your gratitude for His kindness. You do not need to spend five months like Elizabeth did. That is not how she started. Habits are formed bit by bit and continuously. Before you know it, it will become a lifestyle. This spiritual woman knew that her help came from the Lord and she was not disappointed; neither will you nor I be when faced with any crisis. The secret? God's presence.

Fruits of God's Involvement

"Now Elizabeth's full time came that she should be delivered and she brought forth a son. And her neighbours and her cousins heard how the Lord had showed great mercy upon her; and they rejoiced with her." Luke 1:57

Now was the time for the public, for the crowd. It was time to rejoice and accept the celebration from relatives and neighbours. The Lord had honoured her. She had received counsel and wisdom from Him. Her husband had communicated the name of their child to her so there was no dispute or ignorance anywhere. She could not be persuaded to do that which was not right in the eyes of the Lord God who had conquered barrenness for her. He had prepared a table for her in the presence of her mockers and scoffers. She had also received the spiritual capacities to ensure that all that God had designed for the child would be accomplished. When the child was in the womb, he was surrounded by the presence of God through the praying and worshipping of his mother. John had heard the voice of prayer, worship and God's Word and these actually affected him. He could easily respond to the Spirit of God. When the Lord Jesus, the Baptizer came while in the womb of Mary who visited his mother, John too was filled with the Holy Spirit while in his mother's womb and leapt with joy.

I advise pregnant and nursing mothers to make their unborn and young children hear them pray. Read the Word aloud to them. Play or sing songs of worship while they are in the womb or when breast-feeding them. Pray for the milk before you breast-feed. Prophecy on them to their hearing that they belong to God. Pray that they will fit into God's purpose for their lives. It affects the children when they are born and while they are growing.

Elizabeth had limited time to stay with her son. She would have loved to care for, cook for and pamper her only son but had to overcome the agony of seeing him leave home to go to the wilderness where he ate locusts and wild honey. She could not make good clothes for him to wear but was also submitted to seeing him wear clothes made of camel's hair and a leather girdle about his loins – just like the prophet Elijah. She had to let him be what God had spoken of him. She knew God's will for her son and had to let him go.

Many of us do not know what kind of children God has given us, or what God wants or has planned for them to be. Too often we pursue our own desire without asking God to show us how to pray for them so that they'll fulfill God's purpose in their generation. It is not too late. God is still at work and can order the foot-steps of everyone He desires to use. The Lord Jesus says, "My Father is working and I am working." John 5:7 Hand all your children to the Lord today in prayer and the Lord will take over. If you believe in the Bible which says that children are a gift from God, then know that God cannot give us bad gifts. He has a plan for their lives.

Elizabeth the Disciple-Maker

The Bible recommends *"the older women to teach the younger women the ways of the Lord; to be keepers at home, to love their husbands and children, and to be teachers of good things pertaining to holy living. Titus 2:3-5.*Inasmuch as there is the need for women meetings where they can be taught the Word and other practical things pertaining to godliness, there is also the need for one-to-one relationships in which deeper intimacy can be cultivated. Mary found this in Elizabeth whose godly life and devotion to God she admired. Moreso, their current experiences were similar.

Elizabeth's pregnancy was announced by an angel and she was also going to have her first baby, but she had been married for a long time and had also known the Lord longer than Mary. It was through her that Mary received confirmation of the message the angel had given her.

We must understand that Elizabeth did not know about Mary's visit but as she entered, Elizabeth declared,

"And whence is this to me that the mother of my Lord should come to me?"– Luke 1:43

We all need someone who can speak into our lives, someone who can impart spiritual deposits and give us spiritual insight into the things of God; women who have practical life experiences that they have lived through and can share with us. In this way we can be free to open up to them and express the fears and the challenges we are facing. This kind of relationship involves training and periodic companionship.

Mary stayed with Elizabeth for a while because she was about to marry. Elizabeth also needed this relationship with Mary. Unknown to her Mary began carrying the Lord Jesus in her womb as soon as the angel announced that the Holy Spirit will come upon her and the power of the Most High will overshadow her. Upon her entrance then, Elizabeth, this humble woman was influenced by who Mary was carrying and was also filled with the Holy Spirit. She was the second woman to be thus filled and manifested the gift of prophecy.

"Blessed art thou among women and blessed is the fruit of thy womb. Blessed is she that believeth for there shall be a performance of those things which were told her from the Lord" Luke 1:42-45

Until Mary's visit she was only a worshipper and a quiet woman of prayer but suddenly her gift of prophecy became manifest. Prophetic worship flowed to Mary who was moved by impartation and responded in prophetic worship as well something she had never done before.

"My soul doth magnify the Lord and my spirit hath rejoiced in God my Saviour" Luke 1:46.

Spirit had touched spirit in divine connection. Mary was also fully and truly liberated. She entered into her calling and assignment without fear or doubt. Elizabeth's presence helped her enter into a Divine experience. She is now ready to move on and serve God. She was no longer confused. She was now confident that God was with her.

Do you now see why you need such people? You do not just relate with everybody in the same way. Ask the Lord to lead you to someone who can inspire you through the help of the Holy Spirit and lead you increasingly to spiritual maturity in a discipleship relationship. It will lead you to joy, liberty and confidence in your Christian journey. God is there! The Lord Jesus Christ is there! The Holy Spirit is there, but they also want us to touch the lives of the godly people He has released to bless us. You can be an Elizabeth in someone's life or get an Elizabeth in your life. We need one another.

The Need of the Hour: Worshippers

The Lord said to me some time ago, "My need now is for worshippers." We have many warriors but worship is a missing jewel in many Churches because there are few worshippers. This is my personal understanding of who a worshipper is:

1. A worshipper allows God to come down and work in circumstances and situations on her behalf.

2. A worshipper is calm and sweet.

3. A worshipper is at rest because her faith and trust are in God.

4. A worshipper believes that God will always keep His promise.

5. A worshipper is never anxious or worried; she does not take offence at God.

6. A worshipper is always waiting on God to see Him at work.

7. A worshipper is devotional and humble.

8. A worshipper depends on God to defend her.

9. A worshipper carries God's presence wherever she goes.

10. A worshipper enjoys God's presence at all times.

11. A worshipper admires God and is always grateful for everything.

12. A worshipper honours God in her dressing.

13. A worshipper honours God in the way she keeps her home.

14. A worshipper honours God in her service in the Church.

15. A worshipper honours God in the way she treats His servants.

16. A worshipper honours God in the way she relates with other believers.

17. A worshipper considers God's pleasure in everything she does.

18. A worshipper loves God's will and so labours to know it.

19. A worshipper puts God first in her life, not mindful of man's opinion.

20. A worshipper is a woman of the Word, she knows and loves it.

21. A worshipper labours to be filled and remain filled with the Holy Spirit.

She is a woman of the prophetic ministry and her gifts of the spirit are mostly prophecy and faith. She is gifted in hearing the voice of the Lord. God has become her Father in the reality of the word; He is her true Friend, Protector, Provider and Comforter. Her circle of friends is usually very small because she needs much time to spend with God. She is a pursuer of God; she desires His nature, His ways and His emotions. She develops an excellent spirit through her submission to the dealings of God in her life. She never compromises the Word of God because she is mindful of what God is saying. She is always on God's side. She is sensitive to what He is doing or in which direction He is moving at a particular time.

Worshippers are intercessors who seek the will of God and bring it down to earth to be executed as it is in Heaven. They love to see God glorified, the Lord Jesus exalted and the Holy Spirit given His rightful place in the Church and in the Lord's work. They are owned by God and make themselves available to be used by Him in whatever way He chooses. They are in His grip, anointed only for God's instructions and assignments. They are the beloved of God and pursue Christ-likeness. The world and its fashions, lifestyles and pursuits of fame have no power over them. They are overcomers. They know the power of the Cross and the Blood, and have entered into the supernatural power of the Resurrection.

They can never be deceived or misled because God has now become their Wisdom, always giving them counsel and guidance. God fights their battles and keeps them from going astray. They can go nowhere without Him. They can do nothing without Him. They wait for confirmation from Him for everything. They and all that they have belong to God.

Will you be a worshipper? If you already are, please encourage and raise many more like you. If you are not, enroll today. God is waiting for His need to be met by you!
God bless You!

CHAPTER
THREE

JOCHEBED

CHAPTER TWO JOCHEBED

The Bible tells us that Jacob went to Egypt when his son, Joseph was governor during the period of famine which affected the whole earth. It is stated that the number of people that came with him (his family) were 66 excluding the wives of his sons. If we add the eleven wives (Joseph was not there) his whole entourage which entered Egypt was 77 persons. All through the reign of the Pharaoh under whom Joseph was governor, the children of Egypt flourished and increased in number. They filled the whole place because the Lord had multiplied them and made them a mighty army. Of course with time, Joseph and all his brethren in that generation died. Then trouble started. The Bible puts it this way:

"Now a new king arose over Egypt who did not know Joseph."
– Exodus 1:8

This new king, determined to destroy the Israelites, passed a decree that every male child born to a Jewish home or family must be thrown into the River Nile. Only the female children were allowed to live. The fortune and enjoyment of the Israelites changed. They switched to slavery and oppression in contrast to the favourable conditions they had enjoyed when Joseph was alive. There was acute poverty, misery, and hardship as the Egyptian slave masters hardened the working conditions of the Israelites into unbearable suffering. It is in this atmosphere of hostility and wickedness that Jochebed brought forth her third child, a son doomed to succumb to the Pharaoh's decree.

Who is She?

The name Jochebed means 'Jehovah is my Glory'. She was married to Amram and they both were from the priestly family of Levi. Her two other children (Miriam a girl of about eight years old) and Aaron (a boy of about three years) were at home with her to share the plight of losing their baby brother. What a tragedy! Can you imagine a family not able to rejoice or celebrate the birth of a new born baby? There was nothing to be happy about; no consolation anywhere. Her husband was out every day suffering under the yoke of slave-masters. He always came home late, hardly able to carry his battered and tired body. Her tribesmen were under hard labour, each having his own burdens and concerns, and unable to solve the problems of the others. Her two children were still very young. Can you imagine the agony of this woman? She managed to keep the baby from the watching eyes of the Egyptian guards for three months but the crying and wailing of a growing baby could no longer be hidden. What would she do?

Have you ever found yourself in a situation where you cannot get help from anyone or you do not even know what to do? It may not be the same like having to save the life of your child, as in Jochebed's situation. Sometimes it may be something that you cannot share with anyone because they might not understand. Let us see how our sister handled her situation.

"I will not be Pushed Around"

Before anyone makes such a declaration, he must have an anchor. Jochebed was determined that no crocodile would eat her baby. She spent sleepless nights alone figuring out on how to save her baby. Maybe Psalm 27 came to her mind:
"The Lord is my Light and my Salvation. Whom shall I fear? The Lord is the Strength of my life. Of whom shall I be afraid?" (Psalm 27:1).

So she called on Him who is Light, Salvation and Strength; "Lord save my son. Show me what to do Lord!"

She was convinced that her Jehovah had a special place in His heart for her son. It was impossible for God to give her a baby for the sharks to eat. God was good, kind and cared about everything that concerned her. He had seen her carrying her baby for nine months, and had allowed her to go through the pain and agony of delivery. God who saw her through the difficulties could not now give up her baby for an animal to eat. That would have been a reversal of His creative principles for He created animals for us to eat and not vice versa. It can happen in an accident when someone strays unarmed into a wild animal territory, but that was not the case here. In her personal struggles and night vigils with her God, He gave her light on what to do. She received wisdom and a strategy which could only be applied by someone who knew what she was doing.

I would like us to note something here – our sister did not waste her time and energy cursing and insulting Pharaoh who had passed the decree. She refused to sit and wail over her son who was going to die. She did not blame God for allowing His people to suffer under a wicked ruler. She was not even quarrelling with her husband over the issue or blaming him for being weak and uninvolved in this matter. None of these reactions could salvage the situation. Her main concern was to find the solution to this seemingly hopeless situation. She knew that only the One who gave her the gift of a son could rescue him. If she had focused on the negative attitudes, she would have missed to concentrate on God. Never encourage negative thoughts or bitterness to possess you when you want to get God's attention. It will be difficult to hear from Him.

Jochebed now built a basket which I call a mini-Noah's ark. This was for her son's safety. She had heard from God and her faith was released into action. She worked with the confidence of a woman in charge of a situation; full of courage, creativity, wisdom and determination. God was above the laws of Pharaoh. Her God was the owner of the world (Psalm 24:1) and He had provided the solution and showed her the way out! Most probably, her husband did not even know the battles she was fighting or what she was doing. But she had a co-worker in her daughter, Miriam. Together they conspired to embark on this dangerous mission. Jochebed placed the basket in a place where Pharaoh's daughter came to bathe. Then she instructed Miriam to hide somewhere and keep an eye on her baby brother's basket, praying that all would go well.

Sure enough, Pharaoh's daughter saw the basket, and commanded her maid to collect it and bring it to her. The crying baby moved her compassion and she took him out of the basket. Miriam quickly showed up from out of her hiding place and 'innocently' asked if she could find a woman to nurse the baby for her.

Egyptians are highly superstitious. The River Nile was considered a sacred river owned by the gods. The princess therefore concluded that the gods had given her the gift of a son. Joyfully, she accepted Miriam's proposal. You can imagine the speed with which she ran off to call her mother whose heart was panting and waiting to get news from Miriam. The plan had worked. Her son was given to her to nurse in a legal, official and authorized motherhood without fear of the law. The princess named the boy, Moses meaning 'Drawn out of the water'.

Why am I taking time to expose this drama? It is for us to understand how faith works. The Bible says faith comes by hearing and hearing by the Word of God (Romans 10:17). Before you step into an action of faith you must have heard from God. It is not to take a portion of scripture and claim it by faith.

Peter heard Jesus call him to "come" before he stepped on the water and started walking. Abraham heard from God before he carried his only son, Isaac to sacrifice him. Noah could not be stopped by the jeering and mockery of his fellow men when they saw him building an ark to sail on dry land as they presumed; he had heard from God. The apostle Paul could not be stopped from going to Rome even though there was a prophecy that he would be attacked and jailed in Jerusalem; God had told him that he should go to Rome. Jochebed had clearly heard instructions from God during her prayer time. People of faith do the craziest things that sometimes make them look like fools. And as such times, they consult nobody, even their closest relations. What is important to them is that they must do what God has told them to do.

Jochebed is one of those rare women of faith. Faith moved her to put the life of her son in jeopardy. She comes out as a champion. Champions are not stopped by goliaths, mountains or problems. Losers see problems, give excuses, complain, murmur, get angry, become discouraged and finally give up. They are always giving to the negative and full of discouragement.

She did not disclose her scheme to anyone because someone would have discouraged her. She did not wait to attend a prayer meeting and bring her lamentations for the brethren to help her find a solution. This thing was so personal and urgent that she chose to give God an opportunity to demonstrate His sovereignty over the affairs of men. What seemed a tragedy became an outstanding miracle that brought laughter and jubilation in Amram's household. Why? There was a woman who would not allow evil men and evil decrees to run her around and control her children's destiny. A praying woman who was confident in her God had brought all of heaven down into her family. Her God responded in great style. The events were so organized that only God alone could receive the Glory. Halleluya!

Promotion

The faith of Jochebed was God's own faith given to her because she trusted and believed in Him as the answer. The bible says without faith it is impossible to please God. Only God's Divine arrangements produced the drama of Moses' deliverance. How did Jochebed please God? She knew and believed that God is good. He cares and He understands. He loves, protects and fights our battles. She believed what God says He is and refused to accept the devil's lies that God is not interested in what happens to us. Because of her concept of who God is, Her God was pleased with her and promoted her for her loyalty and admiration of Him. Of course, we know that even in practical life, people in authority always promote those who are loyal, who admire them and are close to them, and those who speak well about them. Our Father does it even in an extensive way. He wants us to believe who He is, as we call Him by His names – Jehovah- Jireh, Jehovah-nissi, Jehovah-shammah, etc. That is His nature.

How was Jochebed promoted? See, Pharaoh's daughter did not only give her, her son to nurse but paid her for being her child's nurse. Can you imagine the irony of someone paying you for taking care of your own child? The second point is that poverty was eliminated from her home. Pharaoh's daughter's son could not grow in a dirty environment. Her house was renovated, the outlook of both mother and Miriam who was eventually a maid were changed. She was on Pharaoh's payroll and she became a government worker. There was decent food on their table and officials to guard the environment, just to name a few innovations that characterized Mr. and Mrs. Amram's habitations. That was not all. Jochebed now had access into Pharaoh's palace because from time to time, she had to take the child to see his adopted mother, the princess. There was certainly a royal carriage sent to take them to and from the palace. What a wonder! I will leave you to fill in the other ornaments of her blessings.

Above all these, Jochebed had the glorious privilege of teaching her son the way of the Lord. He knew he was a Jew and a descendant of parents and a tribe who were also Jewish. He was an Israelite and had no blood relation with the Egyptians. She taught him about her God and together with the other two children, Miriam and Aaron; she showed them by example to be devoted to God. This praying woman of faith has her name in the pages of the Holy Book because she produced three great leaders for the people of God:

- Moses – one of the greatest leaders in the history of the bible
- Aaron – a high priest
- Miriam – a prophetess

Do you see why she cannot be forgotten? Her legacy is great. Her name echoes the words of King David;

"My glory and the lifter of my head; I cried unto the Lord with my voice and He heard me out of His Holy hill. He's my Glory and lifter of my heart." Psalm 3:3-4

Jehovah is indeed her glory. The child grew up and became a son in her hands. At the appointed time, when she had deposited spiritual things into him and established his identity, she fearlessly released him into the palace for God to do with Him what He had planned for her son's life. She knew that this child was a son of destiny and only God who had preserved his life could lead him there. She had done her part, finished her own assignment and could let him go. Even today, God is placing little babies in our hands that we should nurture them and give them back to Him. No baby is born to be ordinary. It is the spiritual foundation that a mother imparts in her son or daughter that determines his usefulness in the future.

No matter how long it takes, God will honour the prayers of a devoted mother, orchestrate the journey of her child and establish the child where they will become an ambassador for heaven. They will become an ambassador whether they serve in a government system, private enterprise, the Lord's vineyard or any other professional role. God will always answer. It does not happen overnight. It took many years before Moses, Aaron and Miriam emerged as leaders. The prayers that David prayed for his son Solomon in Psalm 72 were only answered years after David was gone. Keep praying for your children and do not relent.

Reflections and Personal Application

Your crisis or trial may not be like Jochebed's situation. We all face trials of different magnitude and sometimes we wonder how we will get through. Remember, the more you get close to God, the more the devil is after you. However God uses these times of trials to accomplish many things in your life, not necessarily for you to be comfortable. On the contrary, He is more interested in making you holy for without holiness no one can see God. The bible says,

"Every branch in me that beareth not fruit, He taketh away; and every branch that beareth fruit, he purgeth it, that it may bring forth more fruit".– John 15:2

The more you will be used by God, the more He prunes you, purges you and removes the un-wanted things in your life. For sure, the periods during which you are being pruned are not joyful. It is a painful period, sometimes you cry, wondering when it will be all over. It is during times of trials that you learn to endure and never give up. It is just like when a woman is in labour, the pain and agony does not make her give up because she knows and is determined to bring forth her baby. After delivery she forgets the suffering and rejoices to see the new-born child.

So it is, when the Lord has finished the pruning process, the suffering becomes history.

Trials come when God want to refine us and we come out changed. Many believers remain the same year-in, year-out without any change in character or service to God. This is because they evade the cross, run away from any suffering for the Lord's sake, and do not spend any time in God's presence alone with Him or His Word. These are the things that make us change from glory to glory in resembling Christ. Such believers go to church, attend meetings and are satisfied with just hearing messages but never take time to make the word which is taught to become a life experience.

The truth is that the Lord is always with us in every trial. He has experienced pain; in fact He has a doctorate in the school of suffering so He can see us through it all. He says I will never leave you nor forsake you. At the appointed time we always come out victorious. Trials are times of preparation for greater use and fruit-bearing. Until I embrace my trials in an unwavering submission to God, I will not enjoy the good that comes out of it. The bible puts it this way,

"For the time being no discipline brings joy, but seems sad and painful; yet to those who have been trained by it, afterwards it yields the peaceful fruit of righteousness [right standing with God and a lifestyle and attitude that seeks conformity to God's will and purpose]."– Hebrews 12:11 (AMP version).

Jochebed was not the cause of the trial she went through; it just came because of the circumstances of life. Sometimes we can be the cause of our own suffering. In such a case, we just need to repent and ask the Lord to forgive us unto restoration.

Secondly, many of us have faced the situations in which Jochebed found herself. The bible says after the death of Joseph, his brethren and all their generation died, the new Pharaoh (king) did not know Joseph. The children of Israel had their pride and protection in Joseph, their brother and prime minister who also had influence with Pharaoh, the ruler of Egypt. They were secured, had freedom and prospered. When this man died their whole world was shaken and destabilized. It happens in the church too. Most believers who depend on a particular spiritual leader or pastor for security are totally destabilized when he passes away. They had no anchor in the Lord. They backslide, stop serving the Lord, withdraw, look for another church or remain spiritually stagnant. If you are in such a situation, then return to the Lord.

Seek God and know Him as your anchor and security. The governments of nations change and even great leaders sometimes face political instability. God is able to make us stand firm and pray for survival. Churches are not perfect because they are made up of imperfect people so we cease to boast of our churches, ministries or denominations. Our pride should be in our knowledge of God as our security. He is above all governments of the world, spiritual leaders, family heritage, traditions or cultures. God is the solution. He is our anchor.

The Lord is looking for women who can change their homes, environment, society and churches through their devotion and faith in God. If you have to find out faults and things that are wrong in your church, family or nation, you will have a lot to fuss about. But a woman who knows God and has faith believes that God can bring good from a messy situation. Put away every negative attitude and bring solutions by wrestling with God for Divine intervention without blaming anyone. Remember that Jochebed did not utter a word of anger; she did not hate or place blame on Pharaoh or the task masters.

Have the same kind of attitude. Jochebed paid the price of love. Be a mother of the church by praying for God's people. God will reward your love and sacrifice of prayer openly and you will rejoice at the changes in the atmosphere and situation.

She was not the only Jewish mother with children in Egypt but her three children were chosen as leaders. Why? She knew God, trusted Him, grew intimate with Him and trained her children by example of devotion to God. Won't you be one of the solution-bringers? Distinguish yourself and you will be remembered.
Say this prayer with me when the going is hard:

Lord, I will go through this trial so that I will remain bound to You.
I am not angry with You Lord. I do not blame anybody.
Sometimes I am sad, confused and unhappy but I will not quit.
I believe what you say in your Word that in all things You work for the good of those who love you and are called according to your purpose.
I know that good will come out of this trial and I am willing to wait for You.
Sometimes I have doubts, I get worried and anxious Lord, sometimes I even cry.
I ask for Your grace to continue and not relent.
Only You understand what I am facing because You are an experienced sufferer.
You have promised never to leave me nor forsake me.
I have decided that only You will win in this battle.
I know I will come out better than before; I can never be the same after this.
Lord, only You will receive the glory for every benefit and good that will be worked in my life.

Thank You Lord.

Amen!

CHAPTER
FOUR

LYDIA

CHAPTER FOUR LYDIA

Not all women who are remembered in the Word were married, had children or had supernatural experiences. Some of them lived ordinary everyday life, single but happy in their professions and fitted themselves in the norms and cultures of their societies and communities. Lydia was one of such women. In the program of Heaven, the Sovereign Lord, who is no respecter of persons, orchestrates events on earth so that those whom He had ordained from the foundation of the earth are fitted into His plans. The bible puts it this way,

"For we are His workmanship, created in Christ Jesus unto good works, which God hath before ordained that we should walk in them."– Ephesians 2:10

And so sister Lydia's name appears in the pages of God's Holy Book as is mentioned in Acts 16: 14-15, 40.

God as a Master Planner

The apostle Paul had received a call from the Lord through a vision to go to Macedonia. Meanwhile, the Holy Spirit had forbidden and restrained him from going to the places that he desired to go for church planting and preaching of the gospel. A man of Macedonia stood before him in a vision pleading that he should come and help them. That is how Paul and Silas found themselves in Philippi, the capital city of Macedonia.

We must understand that the Holy Spirit has been given to us not only for signs and wonders but also for guidance.

He is the spirit of Truth given to guide us into the will of God. He shall speak to us whatsoever He hears from the Lord. He is always there to direct us on where to go, what to do and His indwelling presence empowers us to obey God. Many believers are not hearing His voice because they are not sensitive to His voice. He is speaking today as He was in the days of Apostle Paul. He can speak to us in a small still voice if we are calm enough. He can give us deep impressions which make us know that He is the one inspiring these impressions.

Paul the Apostle was used to hearing the voice of God because of his constant fellowship with the Holy Spirit through his times of prayer and fasting. He understood where he was directed to go and the result was his encounter with the woman called Lydia. Again, the Holy Spirit was at work in Paul's life so he was directed to go for prayers out of the city by a river side where the women of the city were gathered for one of the women's meetings. What an opportunity! Paul and Silas had a mini-crusade with only women as their audience. The Lord opened one woman's heart to understand the Gospel and receive the Lord Jesus Christ into her life.

It appears that the group of women who knew something about the existence of God had never heard the true Gospel of salvation through Jesus Christ. Even today, there are many women who come together, committed to religious activities, singing hymns of God, reading bible stories and sometimes doing good works to please God. Many of them have never understood the difference between their religious activities and salvation through receiving the Lord into their lives for inward transformation and the new birth experience to become children of God. It appears Lydia had a spiritual need, a vacuum in her spirit that no religious background or activity could fill. God saw her hunger for truth and the Gospel changed her mindset. She realized that something had happened to her. When she received Jesus into her life, she became a different woman.

Her Background

Lydia is spoken of as a business woman, seller of purple material. Purple is a colour of wealth and riches so the materials she sold were not just cheap stuff that anyone could afford to buy. Only the rich people and women of affluence in the city were able to afford her merchandise and do business with her. Consequently she was among the influential and notables in her community; sophisticated in her lifestyle with a big house and workers to sell for her. She also had household servants to do domestic chores and attend to her personal needs. The pathway of suffering did not know her address because she had all she needed. She also had a say in the affairs of the city. Her business opened the way for her to have associations with the dignitaries in the city. Inspite of her busy schedule of business meetings and a lot of travelling to buy good purple material for her customers, she found time to mingle with and be part of the meetings with other women. God honoured her quest for Him and spotted her out for salvation. She became Paul's first convert in Philippi. The Lord had not only pre-destined her for salvation but also purposed her to be a part of the Apostle Paul's ministry in Philippi. God had use of her in His work that He had entrusted to Paul and Silas.

I am Part of His Program

The transformation in Lydia was remarkable. She obeyed the Gospel and submitted herself to water baptism by immersion according to the Scriptures. The joy of salvation was so immense in her that she could not keep it to herself. She shared the good news with her entire household and everyone believed and was baptized. It reminds me of when I received Christ in my life more than forty years ago. It happened when I was living outside my nation; I literally wrote several letters back home to my relatives, friends and even the big Pastor of my denomination telling them all to be born again. I told everyone I met about the love of Jesus, and went into homes and schools to preach the Gospel. It was all so joyful. The experience of the new life in Jesus is not something anyone can hide. Lydia was no exception to the joy of salvation. It had to be shared first to her household. The Lord did not only touch her heart; even her wealth and money were affected. She thought of her big spacious house with many rooms and much food. What could she offer the Lord for what He had done for her? Then that which was in her came out – hospitality. She pleaded with the two missionaries to bless her home with their presence; *"If you have judged me to be faithful to the Lord, come into my house and abide there. And she constrained us."– Acts 16:15*

In other words, she pleaded with them; if you are convinced that I am now a believer like you then please stay in my home. Paul and Silas accepted the offer and her home became the base for their work in Philippi.

Spiritual Impact

Because Lydia offered her home for the missionaries to stay, a house church was started in her home. The missionaries had meetings with new converts teaching them the ways of the Lord, and as many as got saved joined the others in Lydia's home and were established in the Lord. By the time the apostles left Philippi to continue in their missionary journey, the house church had grown and later became a huge congregation with bishops and deacons as we read in Philippians 1. The gift of hospitality goes with love and care. She obviously spent money to make provisions for the needs of her guests, shared love gifts to those who came to her house for fellowship and supported Paul and his team in the missionary enterprise. Because the foundation of the church in her home was giving and loving, the church in Philippi was a giving church. When you read the epistle to the Philippians, it is filled with joy and appreciation. The Apostle Paul says,

"When I departed from Macedonia, no church communicated with me as concerning giving and receiving, but ye only. For even in Thessalonica ye sent once and again unto my necessity."– Philippians 4:15-16

This virtue of the church was imparted from the woman in whose house the church began. She encouraged her congregation to participate in supporting the ministers of the gospel and especially those working as missionaries. By her attitude, she must have also sown a seed of love and unity because Paul constantly mentions this in his letter to them, encouraging them to continue in this way. The letter is characterized by an atmosphere of joy and nostalgia from Paul, desiring to always visit them. His prayers for them were sweet encouraging, comforting and consoling. The church was united and Christ was always exalted. It is one of those churches that were almost free from strife or quarreling. There were miraculous conversions like the Philippian jailer and his household and others who saw the workings of God through Paul. The Lord saved her for such a time as this so that her riches would be rightly used for the promotion of the Gospel. Yes Lydia, the church in Philippi owes its establishment and growth to your generousity and overflow of love.

Personal Reflections

Lydia was a single woman, with no 'distractions' that a husband and children bring. The Word of God puts it this way; *"He that is unmarried careth for the things that belong to the Lord, how he may please the Lord."(1 Cor. 7:32).* I am not saying that marriage is not a good thing. No; God ordained it and it is good. But if you know the Lord and you are single, you find out how you can spend your time to serve Him who saved you while waiting for the day the Lord will give you a husband if you so desire or if He wills it. You do not need to invite men of God to stay in your house. Lydia did it as an emergency and it was a short-lived action. It was God's initiative at that time to distinguish her through her association and partnership with His minister. She was promoted into a woman to be remembered by her identification with a servant of God. God's promotions come in many ways. It is not everyone who must have a distinct call of her own. She would have remained a seller of 'purple' in the world but her name would never have featured in God's Book of Remembrance no matter her financial success and influence. She enrolled in Paul's team, became his co-worker and the Lord lifted her up. She cannot be dissociated from the church in Philippi. She was without doubt a disciple-maker to many and mother of the church.

My sister, do not struggle to establish yourself and do not mingle with the wrong crowd of women who are going nowhere. Do not spend time with those who do not have a purpose in life or those who do not challenge you to do something for the Lord. The people who surround you will either help you grow and move up or pull you down. Tear yourself away from constantly hanging around those who are at your same level or even lower. Touch the lives of those who have spiritual ambition. Allow the Holy Spirit to lead you to the right company.

What is Your Identity?

Child of God, because you have been transferred from the kingdom of darkness into the kingdom of God's dear son, you inherit all the promises in the Word just as anyone else who is God's child. Whether you are male or female, married or unmarried, widowed or divorced, old or young, yes you are what God says you are. You do not have to change your status in order to be used by God. The Holy Spirit resides in you to usher you into God's assignment for your life. He is in the business of aligning us into our callings or restoring us to what we have abandoned. You are what God says you are. Do not let the devil rob you of your identity. When the temptation comes to feel sorry for yourself because you are not married or you a single mother, join me to make these truthful declarations:
God is my Father.

He has given me to Jesus Christ.
I am forgiven.
Christ is my righteousness so I am righteous.
The very breath of God is in me.
I am a dedicated disciple of Jesus Christ.
I am anointed.
I am a tree planted by the riverside.
I am bought by the blood of Jesus.
I am the beloved of God.
I am the apple of God's eye.
I am a child of the covenant.
I am a princess; a daughter of THE KING.
I am from a royal family – The Heavenly Family.
I have royal blood in me.
I am crowned with His favour.
I am surrounded with His goodness and mercy.
I am co-heir with Christ.
I am from a Royal Priesthood.
I am a peacemaker.
I am the salt of the earth.
I am the light of the world.
I am blessed with all spiritual blessings in heavenly places in Christ.
I have been given authority to trample on snakes and scorpions.
Greater is He that is in me that He that is in the world.
I am full of grace and truth.
I carry the whole armour of God.
I am carrying the Holy Spirit and God's power is in me.
God is at work in my life.
God knows me and knows my name.
His is for me and not against me.
I can depend and stand on His word.
He promised never to leave me nor forsake me.
Whenever I call on Him, He will answer.
I am precious in His sight.
My Father is the richest in Heaven and on earth. He owns the gold and silver.
I can never be poor.
Amen!

CHAPTER FIVE

RAHAB

CHAPTER FIVE RAHAB

E ach time I ask someone if they know or have ever heard of the name Rahab, the answer is always the same … "Oh, the harlot in the Bible"! That is what the name connotes in the mind and mouth of everyone. No wonder no parent has ever named their daughter by the name (at least not to my knowledge). They are afraid their daughter will be influenced by the name and become harlots like the original owner. Thank God the One who created her and brought her into this world did not associate her name to her profession. After all, there are many harlots in the world who are called by many decent names like Martha, Ruth or Susan, but are professional harlots. Our professions are a matter of choice or circumstances in life and not because we bear the names we were given by our parents at birth. God looks at our hearts and motives then He decides whether we are usable in His program or not.

Her story is found in the book of Joshua 2: 1-21. She lived in Jericho. Moses had died and the children of Israel, under the leadership of Joshua, had to go through the large fortified city of Jericho on their way to the Promised Land. The city was surrounded by strong high walls with powerful gates, which made entrance and attack impossible. The inhabitants were secure. This is where Rahab and her family – her father, mother, brothers and sisters were staying. From all indications, she neither had a husband nor children and so only her relatives were her family. She was totally committed to her profession without any distractions. Her house was strategically placed on the town wall so that only her window faced the outside of the city making it secure and safe from any invasion. It must have been a very popular residence, known by everybody including the King of Jericho. There was no doubt that men flocked in and out at random both day and night – maybe she was running a brothel, for one woman could not attend to so many men alone. It was her business. But why would the name of such a woman appear in God's Holy Book? Come along with me and let us discover the unique way in which God singled this woman, Rahab, out for prominence.

The Higher Power Overcomes

Joshua had learnt from his mentor, Moses that you don't go into a fight without knowing the strength of your enemy so he sent two of his soldiers to spy on the city. It was a risky venture but because they believed that God was with them, they were unafraid. What baffles me here is the decision of these men of God to dwell in the house of a harlot. Talk of outward appearance and emotional temptations, there was no dispute. Can you imagine if two servants of God are sent to a nation or city to find out how to hold a crusade for Jesus' conquest and they decide that they will stay in the house of a woman known by the whole community as a prostitute? I leave that for you to draw your conclusions. As God would have it, it was His divine arrangement because this woman had been earmarked by her Maker for spiritual impartation. She was there to receive the spies but discovered by her skilled feminine intuition that they were no ordinary men. These were Jews, Israelites and people of God. She sensed and could feel a great power in them. They were surrounded by a holy atmosphere and a divine purity that overcame her sensuality and immorality. Her seductions and feminine attractions could not touch them. They were emotionally fortified beyond her reach and she found herself defeated and afraid. These men were not only physically strong but spiritually powerful. She immediately changed her program. She would serve them, work for them, honor them and do everything to be on their side.

May the Lord continue to raise such men in our days. Join me to pray that the Lord will empower the leaders of today not to lose focus or vision. Pray that they will be able to overcome the wiles of Satan through seductive women who entice men with food, dressing and immoral spirits. Amen!

These spies knew their mission. They knew what they wanted – the city. They were sent and had to go back with a report. They were men who were accountable and under authority. They were not going to be distracted. They were filled with the power of God and totally separated from the atmosphere around them because they were holy. They did not even need to hold a conversation with Rahab. Just their presence broke down her sinful activity and she started testifying.

"I know that the Lord hath given you the land, and that your terror is fallen upon us, and that all the inhabitants of the land faint because of you."– Joshua 2:9

She was speaking out of experience. She herself was terrified. The power of God had touched her. She recognized them as part of those people for whom God was fighting. Rahab sensed danger. She had a choice; either to expose them, report them to the King and have them arrested or take a risk to be on their side and protect them. It appears the power from these men had touched her had stripped her of the passion to continue in her profession. She must have felt a liberty and freedom from the desire to give her body for men to use in exchange for money. She decided to protect their lives. She put her professional skill to action – lies, craftiness and convincing words, and so managed to send away the King's messengers who were sent to look for the spies. She hid them on the roof of her house and covered them with dried stalks in a way that only she herself knew.

The End of My Life

In retrospect, we can say Rahab had come to the end of herself. She was born in Jericho, not by her choice but it was by parental heritage. She no longer wanted what she was doing, no longer wanted to live where she was living, and no longer wanted to be with the people she had grown up with. She wanted to break away and get out but it was if she was in a pit; a prisoner where there was no escape. She had been trapped by a wrong profession, wrong lifestyle and wrong mentality. All these insights came to her as soon as she met the spies from Israel's army. She did not want to continue with her way of life. She knew the story of Israel's God whom these men represented. In fact, the testimonies of God's power in Israel were known to all the nations and fear of the Israelites terrorized everyone.

"For we have heard how the Lord dried up the water of the Red sea for you, when ye came out of Egypt; and what ye did unto the two kings of the Amorites, that were on the other side Jordan, Sihon and Og, whom ye utterly destroyed." – Joshua 2:10

Now was an opportunity to let go of her past. These people of God were still in her house, hidden on top of the roof of her house.

She could not go with them because that would attract attention. Oh, how she wanted to be saved. Also, staying back, she would die because the King of Jericho had no power to protect or save them from the power of Israel's God. She finally decided to align herself with those who could help her out of her present predicament. She approached the men of God (the spies) – a woman used to give and take – and made her proposal.

"I pray you, swear unto me by the Lord, since I have showed you kindness that you will also show kindness unto my father's house, and give me a sure sign: And that you will save alive my father, and my mother, and my brothers, and my sisters, and all that they have, and deliver us from death."

That is a woman of purpose, ingenuity, wisdom and right thinking. There was a call of destiny in her life. Her destiny was calling her out of her pit and bondage. Only the One who knew her destiny could pull her out. By Divine arrangement, God had directed the steps of His messengers to go her way and make contacts. God in His sovereignty will always bring us to our destiny connectors. He knew that there was a woman in Jericho who needed to be pulled out of imprisonment for His usage. She did not only make them promise as an exchange for her kindness but to swear in the name of their God, thus bringing in God into the promise. It was a deal! No turning back, no betrayal and the spies gave her their word as God's name was involved.

Not Me Alone

The most beautiful thing about Rehab's character here is her unselfishness. She was not contented to be saved alone. She included her father, her mother, her brothers, her sisters and everything they had. No member of her family was going to die, she decided. If these men could save her, even though she did not know how the rescue operation would be done, she had developed faith in the power of their God.

It is amazing how many of us who have been saved from sin by the Lord and are born again are happy and contented with our own salvation when our relatives are under bondage. We come to church, sing, dance and testify but have no passion for the salvation of our relatives. Some of us have unsaved fathers, mothers, children and those in our household who have not believed. It is time to stand before the Lord and passionately ask for their salvation.

It is not time to condemn anyone or to give up on anyone. We must do our part to intercede for them. We must plead to the Lord on their behalf that the Lord who saved you will also save them because they are part of you by blood. Take note that it was neither the preaching of the spies, nor their own boasting about the power of God that overcame Rahab's mindset; It was the power of God IN THEM (the spies' lives). Maybe our presence does not reflect God's holiness. We talk about Christ but we do not live Christ. There must be evidence of His character or the power of His Holy Spirit seen in our daily lives. It is time for every one of God's children to become instruments through which God will reach the members of our families with salvation. That is why He picked you out of the many to affect the lives of those around you. He wants us to intercede for our family members so that the scripture will be fulfilled:

"Believe in the Lord Jesus, and you will be saved — you and your household." - Acts 16:31

Do not give God rest. Pray without ceasing. Intercede until He makes your family, your household and all who belong to you a praise unto our God. He always watches over His Word to perform it. It's left for us to co-operate with Him.

The Blood Continues

As for Rahab, the spies did not only give her their word of promise but also revealed to her the strategy through which her protection would come. She let them down by a rope through her window, for her house was built into the city wall and the window was on the wall of the city. They also instructed her to bind a scarlet cord with which she had let them down to her window. The cord was a sign of separation, identification and protection. Scarlet is the color of blood. Just as the blood that was applied on the door posts of the house of the Israelites on the night of the Passover in Egypt saved them from death, the scarlet cord in Rahab and her family's window signified the same protection from death. (See Exodus 12:13).

Do you see the significance of the covenant between the spies and Rahab – the blood? That is why when Joshua and his men were destroying everything and everyone in Jericho, he specifically commanded the spies to go into Rahab's house and bring her out, her family and all their belongings; and so their lives were spared. Rahab's family must have noticed a change in her which made them believe her warning. It was a miracle for all of them to be convinced and follow her into her house knowing the kind of life she was living. God's people had visited and slept in her house and so the presence of God had transformed her life and her priorities had changed. The hand of a loving, merciful and caring Father had stretched out to a heathen prostitute and incorporated her into His family. She became one with His chosen people and nation.

The Family Tree

This time I want us to see God's love in action. Here was a woman living in obvious sin and totally committed to it. There was no one to tell her the truth. On the contrary, she was encouraged to go on by those around her, including her parents. God singles her out for salvation and orchestrates events to locate her in her heathen environment.

"Before I formed you in the womb I knew you, and before you were born I separated and set you apart." - Jeremiah 1:5

Only God who owns the world and everyone in it can locate those whom He has fore-ordained unto salvation regardless of the pit of sin in which they find themselves or the mess they have made of their lives. Human beings tend to give up on others who, according to their judgment, are worthless, useless and a bad case; not so our Father who is in Heaven.

He says in Acts 17:30 that He winks at the times of ignorance. God disregarded Rahab's sinful years of ignorance because He already had a place for her in His itinerary. Her decision was total and unwavering. It was a beautiful risk. She turned her back on her culture, her language and her people into the unknown. Like Ruth the Moabite, Naomi's daughter-in-law, God fitted her into a people of a strange tradition and lifestyle. She learnt the ways of God. The bible says she dwells in Israel until this day. How?
Rahab travelled with the children of Israel through the desert into the Promised Land during those forty years. Her name appears in the genealogy of the family of the Lord Jesus.

"Salmon the father of Boaz, whose mother was Rahab, Boaz the father of Obed, whose mother was Ruth, Obed the father of Jesse, and Jesse the father of King David."– Matthew 1:5

** We all remember Mary the mother of the Lord Jesus had her lineage from King David.

Rahab could never get married while she was in Jericho but she became a Jew by marriage and had a son who was a relative of the Lord in the flesh. The favor of the Lord followed her and she became an ancestress of the Messiah. What a wonder and a demonstration of the uniqueness of the ways of the Lord God. God's love diminishes all our deficiencies. Hallelujah!

God never changes but He is always changing people, things and situations. The Bible is full of imperfect people, terrible sinners and confused and purposeless people who were transformed by God's power. Even today, He is not looking for perfect women (if there are any) but those He can perfect and then fit into their destiny. Are you willing?

Like Rahab there must be radical separation from the past. There are things in our past or hangovers from the past to which we are still clinging. It will be difficult for God to fit you in your destiny if you refuse to let go. You do not need to run from one city or village to another. It is God who works things out for us when we truly surrender and come to the end of ourselves. God is waiting.

Amen!

A Message to Praying Women

A message given to a team of praying and worshipping women after the funeral of a great and well-known servant of God.

My children (daughters)

I am a Father

As a Father, I have come down to visit you

As a Father, I have come to make straight the crooked way

As a Father, I have come to bring light where there is darkness.

And as a Father, I have come to bring comfort where there is sorrow.

As a Father, I have come to uplift the fallen

As a Father, I have come to bind the broken hearts

I only need your hearts

And I will have my way

I have come that you may know the peace that comes only from ME.

Be calm and learn to wait and listen to ME.

I will not leave you

I will not forget you

My word is in you, in your life

My peace I leave with you all.

(Sunday 27th October, 2013, 7:20a.m).

CPSIA information can be obtained
at www.ICGtesting.com
Printed in the USA
FSHW020725050221
78261FS